W9-AET-867

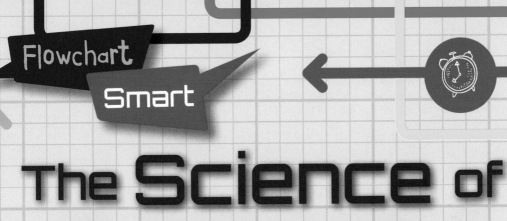

Flowchart Smart

The Science of
FORCES

Mary Colson

Gareth Stevens
PUBLISHING

Please visit our website, **www.garethstevens.com**.
For a free color catalog of all our high-quality books,
call toll free 1-800-542-2595 or fax 1-877-542-2596.

Cataloging-in-Publication Data

Colson, Mary.
The science of forces / by Mary Colson.
p. cm. — (Flowchart smart)
Includes index.
ISBN 978-1-4824-4135-2 (pbk.)
ISBN 978-1-4824-4136-9 (6-pack)
ISBN 978-1-4824-4137-6 (library binding)
1. Force and energy — Juvenile literature. I. Colson, Mary. II. Title.
QC73.4 C65 2015
531—d23

First Edition

Published in 2016 by
Gareth Stevens Publishing
111 East 14th Street, Suite 349
New York, NY 10003

© 2016 Gareth Stevens Publishing

Produced for Gareth Stevens by Calcium
Editors: Sarah Eason and Harriet McGregor
Designers: Paul Myerscough and Emma DeBanks

Cover art: Shutterstock: Denkcreative, Lineartestpilot.

Picture credits: Shutterstock: Andrey Armyagov 24–25, Claudio Bertoloni 1, 21cr,
Bikeriderlondon 6–7, Andrew Burgess 20–21, Fotos593 12–13, Filip Fuxa 38–39, Warren
Goldswain 6b, Hellen Grig 41tr, IM_photo 18–19, Irin-k 33t, Jabiru 4–5, JLRphotography
28–29, Jenny Lilly 40–41, Luciano Mortula 15t, Nagel Photography 13b, Ostill 44–45,
Jose Antonio Perez 26–27, Samot 9t, Stefan Schurr 27b, Seqoya 8–9, SpeedKingz 34–35,
Vicspacewalker 29r, Tom Wang 14–15, Christopher Wood 32–33.

Printed in the United States of America

CPSIA compliance information: Batch #CW16GS: For further information contact Gareth Stevens, New York, New York at 1-800-542-2595.

Contents

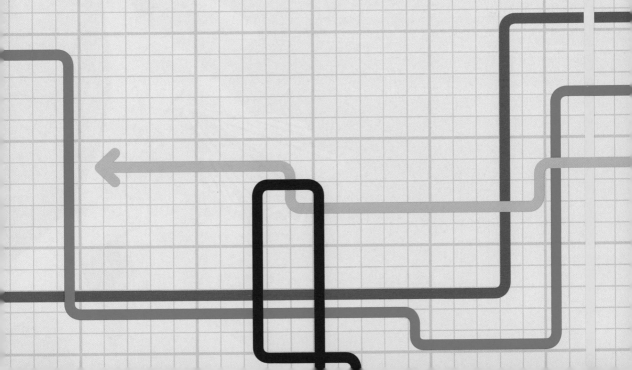

Chapter 1
The Power of Forces

Forces are some of the most powerful things in the universe, but you cannot see them. They're all around us and you can't even feel them, but you can sometimes feel their effects. A force is a push or a pull. When you push or pull an object, you apply force to the object. Forces can make things speed up, slow down, move forward or backward, twist, rise or fall, or stay still.

You use forces every day. In the morning, you get up, get dressed, and have breakfast. You might switch on a light, open a door, turn on the shower, rub yourself dry with a towel, pour cereal into a bowl, and lift a spoon. All these actions require different forces to make them possible. In humans and other animals, muscles produce the force to move body parts. On a much larger scale, planets, stars, and moons in the solar system encounter far more powerful forces.

This book explores the forces around us every day. It explains how forces work and how they move an object or hold materials together, and helps you understand how forces are a part of our existence. You will also learn that without forces, life itself would be impossible.

Roller coasters speed downhill and around corners. You can feel the effects of forces on your body as the track twists and turns.

Balanced Forces

Once an object is moving, it continues to move until another force makes it speed up, slow down, change direction, change shape, or stop. Forces combine to create a bigger force. Imagine two horses harnessed together to pull a cart. They pull a cart more quickly and easily than a single horse because they are combining their forces.

To make something move, one force must be stronger than another. In a tug-of-war, if two teams are pulling in opposite directions with equal force, there is balance. The rope does not move. This balance is called equilibrium. Balanced forces do not cause a change in motion. They are equal in size and opposite in direction.

Unbalanced forces are not equal in size and direction. When one force is stronger than another we get an unbalanced force. We use unbalanced forces to move objects, to speed up or slow down, and to cause a moving object to stop or change direction.

The child that is closest in this photograph is heavier than the one that is farther away. The forces are unbalanced and the seesaw moves.

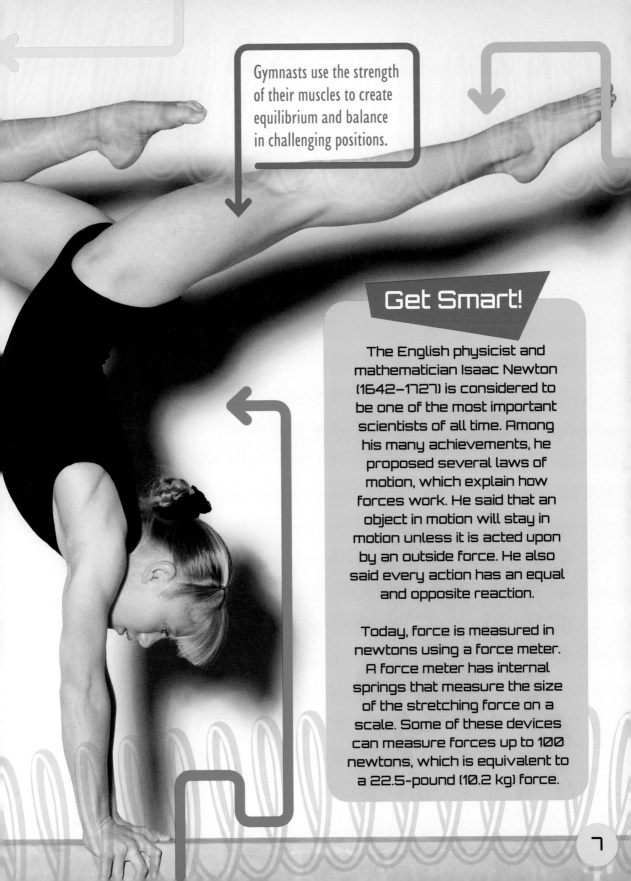

Gymnasts use the strength of their muscles to create equilibrium and balance in challenging positions.

Get Smart!

The English physicist and mathematician Isaac Newton (1642–1727) is considered to be one of the most important scientists of all time. Among his many achievements, he proposed several laws of motion, which explain how forces work. He said that an object in motion will stay in motion unless it is acted upon by an outside force. He also said every action has an equal and opposite reaction.

Today, force is measured in newtons using a force meter. A force meter has internal springs that measure the size of the stretching force on a scale. Some of these devices can measure forces up to 100 newtons, which is equivalent to a 22.5-pound (10.2 kg) force.

The Effects of Friction

Friction is a force that prevents two surfaces from moving across each other. When you hit a baseball or roll a ball along the ground, friction opposes the motion, and eventually slows or stops the ball. Friction does not only exist between two solid surfaces. Think about a boat on water—the water rubbing against the bottom of the boat slows it down. In a similar way, when riding a bicycle fast downhill, your body and the bike rub against the air, which slows you down.

The strength of the force of friction depends on the surfaces rubbing together. If the surfaces are smooth, there will be less friction than if the surfaces are rough. You slide a long way on ice because the ice is extremely smooth and there is little friction. Friction can also generate heat. On a cold day, you rub your hands together to keep warm. It is the force of friction between the surfaces of your hands that makes them warm up.

A camel's feet are flat and wide. The large area increases the friction between the foot and the sand. This helps the camel to grip the sand better and keep it from sinking down into the sand.

The soles of your shoes grip the ground as you walk. Friction causes this grip, whether you are walking on a sidewalk, sand, grass, or gravel. On a very smooth surface, such as ice, there is less friction and the soles of your shoes may not have enough grip to keep you from falling over.

Tractors have huge tires with lots of tread. This increases friction on muddy ground, and keeps them from getting stuck. In contrast, professional cyclists use very thin, smooth tires called slicks to minimize friction and grip, and help them move as fast as possible.

Skiers wax the bottom of their skis to reduce the friction between the skis and the snow, which allows them to travel faster.

Get flowchart smart!

9

Balanced and Unbalanced Forces

Follow this flowchart to take a look at how balanced and unbalanced forces work in a seesaw.

An empty seesaw is a level plank balanced on both sides of a pivot. The forces acting on both ends of the seesaw are equal.

When somebody sits on one end of the seesaw, the forces become unbalanced.

If the second person is heavier than the first person, the seesaw will be unbalanced again. The lighter person will be on the higher end of the seesaw.

The unbalanced forces cause a change in motion, and one end of the seesaw moves down.

If a second person of the same mass as the first sits on the other end of the seesaw, the forces will again be balanced. The seesaw will return to the horizontal position.

Flowchart

Smart

Chapter 2
Forces That Shape Earth

Every day, all over the world, forces change planet Earth. High above the surface, deep underwater, and far underground, forces are at work. The downward force of the atmosphere and the movement of ocean currents cause Earth to wobble and shift by approximately 23 feet (7 m) every 400 days as it spins on its axis. We don't notice this wobble, but we do notice other forces that impact the landscape and the weather, too.

Some of the most powerful natural forces that shape Earth's surface are volcanoes. A volcano is a hole in Earth's crust, which is the rocky outer shell of the planet. Often, a volcano is a tall mountain, but it can also be a large, low mound. Inside a volcano is a chamber of molten rock called magma. When the pressure inside the magma chamber becomes too great, it pushes up through the volcanic vent. Once the magma erupts through Earth's surface, it's called lava. A river of red-hot lava can scar a landscape very quickly, burning trees, buildings, and crops in its path.

Get Smart!

Volcanoes come in all different shapes and sizes. The force of a volcanic eruption can also vary. Scientists called volcanologists measure the strength of a volcanic eruption using the Volcanic Explosivity Index (VEI). This scale runs from 0 to 8. A level "8" eruption is "mega-colossal," producing thousands of cubic miles of lava, an ash cloud more than 15 miles (25 km) high, and causing widespread devastation to the environment. Huge quantities of ash released into the atmosphere would block the sunlight, altering Earth's climate for many years.

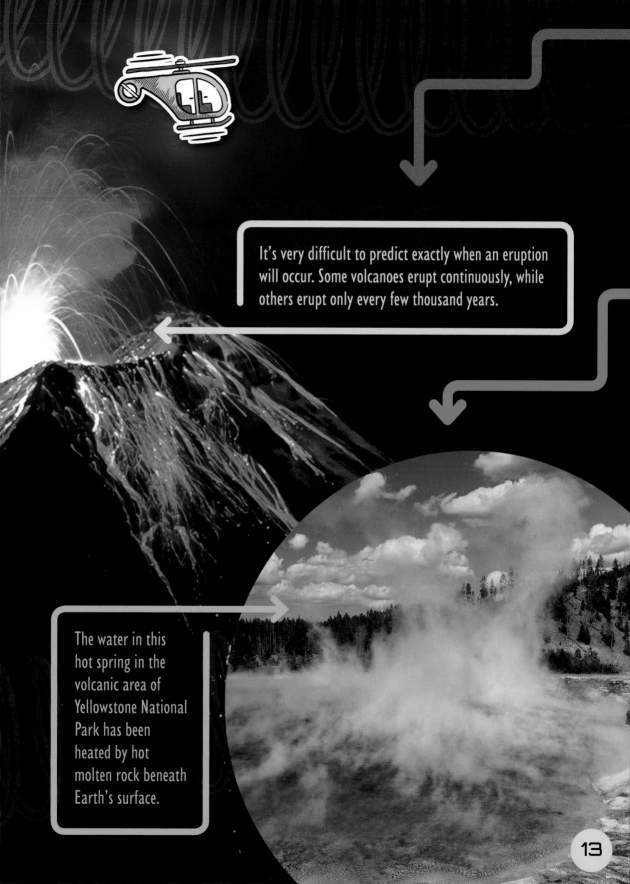

It's very difficult to predict exactly when an eruption will occur. Some volcanoes erupt continuously, while others erupt only every few thousand years.

The water in this hot spring in the volcanic area of Yellowstone National Park has been heated by hot molten rock beneath Earth's surface.

Tectonic Forces

Earth's surface is made up of massive sections of rock called tectonic plates. The plates move constantly and push slowly past, toward, or away from each other. As the plates move, forces are exerted on themselves and each other. Sometimes, the pressure between two plates builds up and is suddenly released as the plates move past one another. This creates powerful waves of energy that we feel as an earthquake. Every year, more than 1 million earthquakes shake Earth's surface.

Earth's plates move at different speeds and in different directions. When plates pull apart from each other, magma rises up from below Earth's surface and forms new crust. When plates push toward each other, the edges of the plates are forced upward and can form mountain ranges. When the plates try to slide past each other horizontally, they often lock and then suddenly release, causing an earthquake. The San Andreas Fault in California is the boundary between the North American and Pacific plates, which move in this way. From the air, the fault line looks like a huge scar across the landscape.

Earthquakes can quickly and dramatically scar natural landscapes and man-made structures, such as this highway.

In San Francisco, where there is a high risk of earthquakes, many tall buildings are earthquake-proof. They have wide bases and are designed to bend and flex like a wave.

Get Smart!

It's not easy to predict earthquakes, and very often they occur without warning. Scientists called seismologists study earthquakes. They use devices called seismometers to help them predict the timing and measure the strength of an earthquake. Seismometers pick up vibrations in Earth's crust. An increase in vibrations might indicate an impending earthquake. Earthquakes are measured on the Moment Magnitude Scale. A magnitude "8" earthquake can totally destroy communities near the epicenter.

Get flowchart smart!

What Forces Cause Volcanoes to Erupt?

Follow the flowchart to examine what happens during a volcanic eruption.

Deep inside a volcano is a vast magma chamber. This is a reservoir of red-hot molten rock.

Gases and rocks ripped loose from inside the volcano are also thrown up into the atmosphere.

The lava and rocks fall back to Earth as dust, ash, and pumice.

When the magma rises in the chamber, the pressure inside it increases.

The pressure forces magma up through weak points called "vents" in the volcano's solid rock.

When the magma reaches the surface, it is known as lava and erupts out of the volcano.

Flowchart

Smart

Chapter 3
Forces in Air and Water

Air has weight and exerts pressure on everything it touches. On the surface of Earth we are essentially at the bottom of a large pool of air. We call this air the atmosphere. It is the weight of the atmosphere pushing down on Earth that gives us atmospheric pressure. Atmospheric pressure is often measured using a barometer. The closer to the surface of the planet, the greater the atmospheric pressure. As you move upward, away from Earth's surface, the atmospheric pressure drops because there is less air pushing down on you.

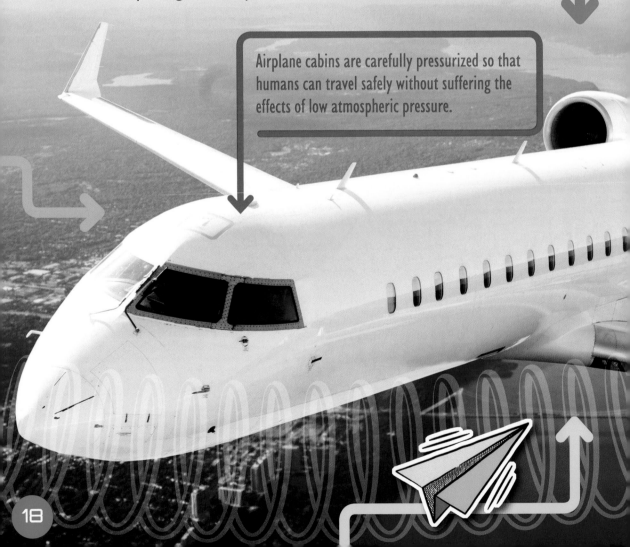

Airplane cabins are carefully pressurized so that humans can travel safely without suffering the effects of low atmospheric pressure.

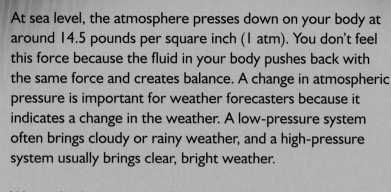

At sea level, the atmosphere presses down on your body at around 14.5 pounds per square inch (1 atm). You don't feel this force because the fluid in your body pushes back with the same force and creates balance. A change in atmospheric pressure is important for weather forecasters because it indicates a change in the weather. A low-pressure system often brings cloudy or rainy weather, and a high-pressure system usually brings clear, bright weather.

Water also has weight and can exert a force. In a swimming pool, water presses on all parts of your body. The deeper you move below the surface of the water, the greater the pressure change. If you dive down to the deep end of a swimming pool, you might feel this pressure in your ears. For every 33 feet (10 m) you go beneath the surface of the water, the pressure increases by 14.5 pounds per square inch (1 atm). The human body can't cope with the high pressure deep beneath the surface of the oceans. The water pressure causes any space that's filled with air, such as the lungs, to collapse.

Get Smart!

Pressure is a force applied over a specific area. If a force is applied to a small area, the pressure is great; if the same force is applied to a larger area, the pressure is lower. Blaise Pascal (1623–1662) was a French mathematician. Among his many achievements, he experimented with atmospheric pressure and how it can be estimated in terms of weight. Pressure can be measured in pascals in honor of his groundbreaking work.

Forces: Up, Down, and Sideways

Forces can push or pull in any direction. When something pushes down on water, the water pushes back up. The force of water pushing back is called upthrust. When you're in the ocean or a pool, press a ball down into the water. The resisting force that you can feel is upthrust. An object in water weighs less than it does in the air. This is because the upthrust of the water cancels out some of the gravitational force pulling the object down. The size of the upthrust force in water depends on the amount of water displaced (pushed out of the way). When upthrust is equal to or greater than the object's weight, the object will float. If the upthrust is less than the object's weight, the object will sink.

Penguins have pointed beaks, smooth feathers, and a streamlined shape. They experience little drag and can swim very fast.

An object moving through air or water is slowed down by the air or water. This force is called drag. Boats are streamlined, which means they have pointed bows and smooth sides to reduce drag and travel through the water as fast as possible. The larger the surface area of the boat, the bigger the resistance, so a ship creates more drag than a sailboat.

Aerodynamics is the science that studies the interaction between air and the solid bodies moving through it. Think about some of the man-made and natural shapes that travel through air. Rockets, planes, arrows, and bullets are all streamlined, or aerodynamic. They have a smooth, slim shape that offers the least resistance to the air, and can therefore travel at high speeds. In the natural world, birds have aerodynamic shapes to help them fly.

Racing cyclists wear tight clothing to create a more streamlined shape, reduce drag, and travel faster.

Get flowchart smart!

How to Use Water Forces

Use this flowchart to take a look at the forces at work when a person water-skis.

The water-skier rests in the water with the tips of the skis above the water's surface. The water-skier holds on to a handle at the end of a rope attached to a speedboat.

The water-skier leans backward slightly to balance the pull of the boat.

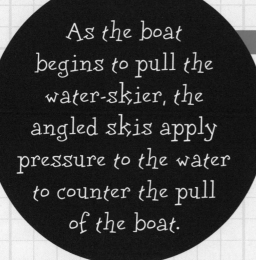As the boat begins to pull the water-skier, the angled skis apply pressure to the water to counter the pull of the boat.

The water is pushed downward by the bottoms of the skis.

The acceleration of the boat and the upward angle of the skis creates an upward force that lifts the water-skier out of the water and into a standing position.

Flowchart

Smart

Success

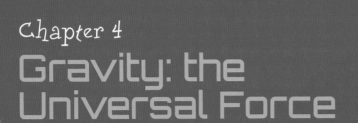

Chapter 4
Gravity: the Universal Force

Gravity affects everything on Earth. It is the force that holds people and all objects on the surface of the planet. If you throw a ball up into the air, the force of gravity slows it down and causes it to fall. The atmosphere and oceans are kept in place by the force of gravity. Without it, the atmosphere would drift off into space and life on Earth would be impossible.

All objects exert gravity on their surroundings, and the strength of their gravity depends on their mass. The moon has a smaller mass than Earth, which is why its force of gravity is less. The astronauts who landed on the moon wore heavy spacesuits. These suits felt much heavier on Earth than they did on the moon. Jupiter is the largest planet in the solar system. Its pull of gravity is stronger than Earth's. It would take more force to walk, run, or jump on Jupiter. The world record for the long jump on Earth is more than 26 feet (8 m). On Jupiter, it would be around only 10 feet (3 m).

On a spacewalk, an astronaut experiences no gravitational force. As a result, the spacesuit feels far less cumbersome than it does on Earth.

Get Smart!

An object's weight and its mass are two different things. The mass of an object is the amount of matter in the object. You have a mass that is made up of your bones, muscles, fluids, and other body parts. Your mass does not change, no matter where you are in the world, because there's still the same amount of you. However, your weight changes depending on your location. Weight is a measure of how strongly gravity pulls on an object. If you weigh yourself at the equator, you will weigh slightly less than at the North Pole, where there is a stronger gravitational pull.

Forces in Space

In space, the stars, moons, and planets keep their positions and orbits as a result of gravity. In the seventeenth century, Isaac Newton realized that gravity on Earth is the same force that keeps the moon orbiting Earth, and all the planets moving around the sun. But how does this force work?

Every object in the universe that has mass exerts a gravitational pull, or force, on every other mass. Humans have some gravitational pull because we have mass, but we are tiny in comparison to Earth or Mars, which have enormous masses. Earth has enough gravitational pull to hold the atmosphere in place around the planet, but smaller objects in space, such as Pluto, may not have enough gravitational pull to hold an atmosphere. The sun is 850,000 miles (1.37 million km) wide—more than 100 times wider than Earth. It has a huge mass and a very strong gravitational pull. The sun's pull is so powerful that it holds all the planets in our solar system in their orbits around it.

The gravitational pull of a planet also varies depending on the planet's density. Neptune has 17 times Earth's mass, but it is also far larger. This means that it has a low density, and as a result its gravitational pull is only slightly greater than Earth's.

A spaceship needs a lot of force to help it reach the speed required to break free from Earth's gravitational pull. The orange fuel tank will be jettisoned once it has helped the rocket into space.

Get Smart!

Space rockets need a lot of power to escape Earth's gravitational force. The speed at which they must travel to leave Earth's atmosphere is called the escape velocity. A rocket accelerates to 25,000 miles (40,230 km) per hour to get into orbit above Earth's atmosphere. The farther away from the center of Earth an object is, the lower the pull of gravity.

A high jumper must generate enough upward force in order to briefly counteract Earth's gravity and jump over the pole.

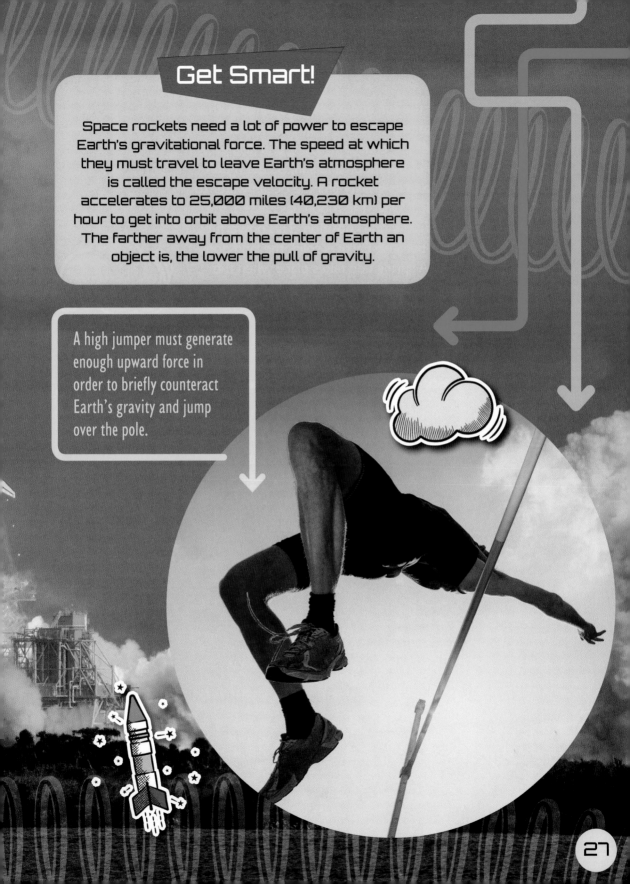

Tides and Waves

The gravitational forces of the sun and moon, combined with the rotation of Earth, cause tides in Earth's seas and oceans. These large bodies of water are constantly rising and falling depending on the position of the moon and sun. As the moon passes overhead, the force of its gravity lifts the ocean water to form a bulge or a "high tide." Once the moon has passed, the water level falls back to its "low tide" position. This powerful force affects land too, but because Earth is solid, the land does not move as dramatically. A spring tide takes place when the moon, sun, and Earth are in a line. The gravity of the moon and sun combines and pulls in the same direction to create an unusually high and low tide on Earth.

As a wave approaches the shore, the bottom of the wave slows down as it meets solid ground. The top part of the wave continues to move forward and eventually tips over as the wave breaks.

Surfers, sailors, and bodyboarders use the force of the waves for their leisure activities. But what is a wave and how do its forces work?

A wave is a moving disturbance that travels through space and matter. As it moves, it transfers energy from one place to another. If you throw a stone into a pond, you can see waves in the form of ripples. If you go to the shore, you can see large waves roll in and move back out.

In water, waves are called transverse waves. This is because the disturbance moves at right angles to the direction of the wave. In the oceans, water moves up and down as the wave passes horizontally. Ocean waves are generated by wind moving across the water's surface. Occasionally, a powerful earthquake on the ocean floor generates a massive tsunami.

The Dead Sea is extremely salty. This makes its water very dense and gives it more upward force than normal seawater. It is a smaller body of water than an ocean, and has smaller waves.

Get flowchart smart!

Launching Rockets

Find out how rockets overcome Earth's gravity, using a flowchart.

A rocket's engines are started and hot gases fire downward toward Earth, creating an enormous force.

This produces an equal yet opposite force that pushes the rocket upward. This is called thrust.

Once the rocket is 62 miles (100 km) from Earth, it has entered space.

The rocket must travel at approximately 7 miles (11 km) per second to escape Earth's gravity. This is the escape velocity and is equivalent to a speed of 25,000 miles (40,230 km) per hour.

Most of the rocket's fuel is used to achieve the required escape velocity.

When a tank of fuel is used up, it is released from the rocket. This makes the rocket lighter and means it needs less force to travel onward.

Flowchart Smart

Chapter 5
Magnetic Force

A magnet is a piece of metal that attracts another metal. The force it uses to do this is called magnetism. You can't see this force, but you can see its effects. The area around a magnet is called a magnetic field. If you place an object in a magnetic field, it will be affected by the magnet. Test it out for yourself. Pick up a fridge magnet and slowly move it toward a refrigerator. As you approach the refrigerator, you will feel the magnetic attraction of the magnet. This means the refrigerator is within the magnetic field of the magnet. The pull will be strongest when the magnet is very close to the refrigerator.

Earth's magnetic north and south poles are located very close to its geographic North and South Poles. Compass needles line up in a north–south orientation between the two poles.

Get Smart!

Deep in space, some objects have a magnetic force many billions of times greater than any on Earth, or elsewhere in the solar system. Scientists use special telescopes to learn about mysterious "magnetars." These phenomena were once gigantic stars, but they have since collapsed and exploded in a supernova. What remains is the core of a star, which is very dense and highly magnetic.

Bees, dolphins, lobsters, and pigeons have tiny magnets in their bodies that enable them to navigate.

Nickel and iron are metals that are magnetic. At the very center of Earth is an inner core of liquid iron. This makes Earth behave like a giant magnet. All magnets, including Earth, have two poles—north and south. Opposites attract, which means that the north pole of one magnet is attracted to the south pole of another. If two north poles or two south poles come together, there is no magnetic pull between them. Instead, they will push apart. This is called repulsion.

Earth's magnetic field protects the planet from radiation and damaging particles from the sun. The magnetic field acts like a shield that deflects these harmful particles back out into space.

Using Magnetic Forces

You might be surprised by how many uses there are for magnets in everyday life. For example, purses, cell phone cases, and bags often close using magnets. Kitchen cabinets and storm doors may also close with magnets. Magnetic paper clip holders can help keep desks tidy. Fridge magnets hold pictures, grocery lists, certificates, and dozens of other items. Household recycling is even sorted using magnets. Recycling centers separate magnetic materials, such as steel, from other waste. Magnets are found inside televisions, computers, doorbells, and music entertainment systems.

Superfast maglev trains use magnetism to travel at incredible speeds of up to 340 miles (550 km) per hour. Maglev means "magnetic levitation" or "lifted up by magnets." Magnetic repulsion between electromagnets in the track and the underside of the train lift the train, which appears to float above the track. There is no friction between the train and the rails, so it can travel very fast.

Doctors use magnets to look inside patients' bodies. The patient lies inside a magnetic ring in a Magnetic Resonance Imaging (MRI) scanner. The magnet is very powerful so any metallic objects, such as keys or watches, must be removed before the magnet is turned on. MRI scans create very detailed images of your internal organs, so doctors can see whether there is any damage or disease. MRI scanners can study the brain to detect which part of your brain you use for different activities, highlight any areas of brain damage, and detect changes in the brain as the patient experiences different emotions.

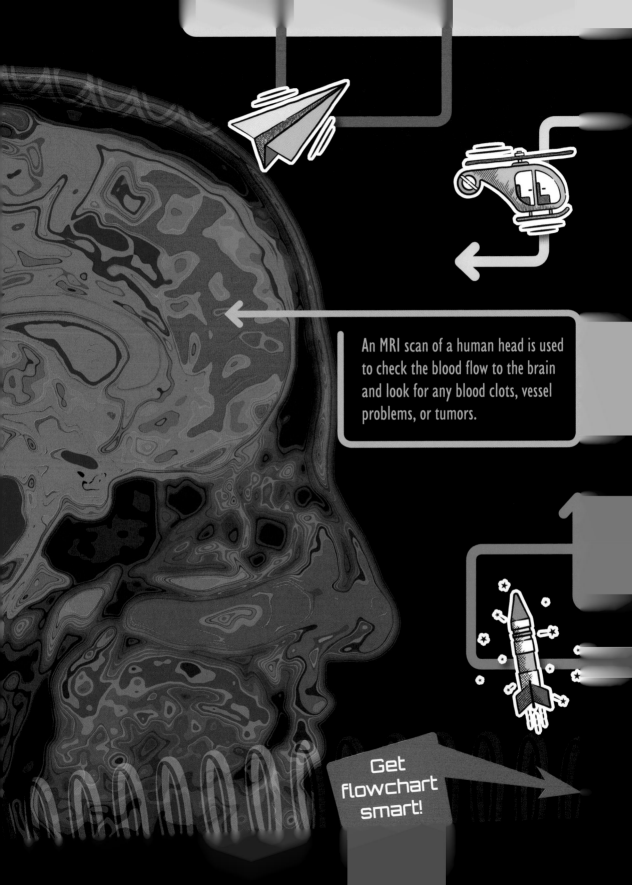

An MRI scan of a human head is used to check the blood flow to the brain and look for any blood clots, vessel problems, or tumors.

Get flowchart smart!

How Magnets Work

Follow the flowchart to examine magnets and their magnetic fields.

Magnets are objects that produce an area of magnetic force called a magnetic field.

Magnetic poles behave differently. Opposite poles attract (pull toward each other) while like poles repel (push away).

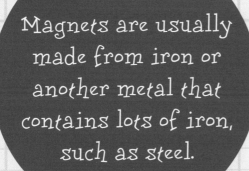

Magnets are usually made from iron or another metal that contains lots of iron, such as steel.

A magnet attracts other objects that are made of iron, or contain iron. This invisible force is called magnetism.

A magnet has *two* poles: *the north* pole and *the south* pole. The magnet is strongest or has the most force at its poles.

Flowchart

Smart

SUCCESS

Chapter 6
Making Forces Work

For thousands of years, humans have known the importance of forces. The mighty monuments of the ancient world, such as the Acropolis in Greece and the pyramids in Egypt, could only have been built using an understanding of forces. Today and in ancient times, simple machines, such as levers, were extremely useful. A lever is a solid bar that rests on a pivot and is used to lift loads. The user exerts a small amount of force on one end of the lever in order to generate a much greater force at the other end.

A pulley is another simple machine. It consists of one or more wheels and a rope. A load is attached to one end of a rope, which is then passed around the edge of a wheel. A groove in the wheel keeps the rope in place. Pulleys change the direction of a force. If you pull down on the rope, it lifts the load. Clotheslines and flagpoles use pulleys. Movable pulleys provide us with a mechanical advantage. They allow us to lift objects that would normally be too heavy. In the construction industry, tower cranes are used to raise very heavy loads. These enormous cranes use balanced and unbalanced forces to keep them upright. They also use pulleys, wheels, and gears in their motors to winch objects high into the air.

Get Smart!

The stone blocks used to build the Egyptian pyramids 4,500 years ago weigh many tons. They are far too heavy to have been carried to the top of the structures. Many historians believe that pulleys and ramps were used to lift the stones, but no one knows for sure. No one has ever discovered any evidence of the infrastructure needed to build the pyramids.

Stonehenge was built 4,000 years ago. The stones came from a quarry nearly 250 miles (402 km) away. They may have been dragged on rollers or sledges and then transported by water.

Forces and Shapes

Imagine a piece of clay. Think about rolling it, twisting it, pushing it, and pulling it into a different shape. You might make a vase, a bowl, or a figure of a person. You exert a force on the clay to make it change shape. Some shapes are stronger than others and require greater force in order to be bent or changed. Scientists, designers, architects, and engineers use the knowledge of a material's strength to create lasting objects, from small items of furniture to towering skyscrapers.

Get Smart!

Next time you look at a building or a bridge, notice the use of circles and triangles. These two shapes are very strong and can bear the heaviest loads. Suspension bridges, such as the Golden Gate Bridge in San Francisco, use triangles. Thousands of years ago, the ancient Romans and Greeks knew about the strength of circles and triangles—these shapes are visible in many ancient buildings. The next strongest shape is an arch, which was used to build many old cathedrals and bridges.

All solid structures and objects have a shape. The shape must be strong enough to serve the object's purpose. For example, in the natural world, a feather's shape serves many purposes, including helping birds to fly and keeping them warm. Spider webs have a specific shape that helps a spider catch its prey. At home or at school, a piece of paper needs enough strength to be written on. A pen must not collapse when it's held. Larger objects, such as cars, bridges, carnival rides, and airplanes, need the best shape to support and protect their loads.

The Brooklyn Bridge in New York City uses strong shapes like triangles and arches to support the suspension cables and the deck.

Spider webs are shaped to withstand huge forces. If a strand of the web is broken, the overall strength of the web increases rather than decreases.

Get flowchart smart!

How Cranes Use Forces

Let's take a look at how cranes are constructed and how they raise loads using forces by following this flowchart.

The base of a crane is fixed securely to concrete on the ground. The tower is built using many triangle shapes for strength.

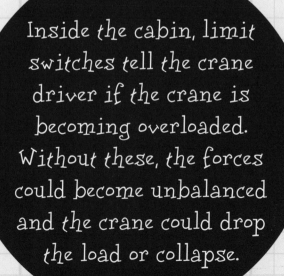

Inside the cabin, limit switches tell the crane driver if the crane is becoming overloaded. Without these, the forces could become unbalanced and the crane could drop the load or collapse.

The load is suspended from a horizontal jib (arm). A trolley runs along the jib to move the load.

A motor and gears are located in the machinery arm. The counterweights, which help balance the crane, are also here.

If the load is lifted near the center of the crane, the crane can lift more weight. If the load is lifted at the farthest end of the jib, away from the center, the crane can only lift a lighter load.

The motor lifts the load using the gears.

Flowchart Smart

Feel the Force

We may not be able to see forces, but we can certainly feel their effects. Forces shape our very existence. We couldn't move, talk, eat, sleep, or even breathe without forces. There would be no atmosphere around the planet and life on Earth would simply not be possible.

For millennia, people have used forces to create amazing structures that we still marvel at today. Scientists and engineers use their knowledge of forces to explore space, develop new technologies, and generate clean energy. Space rockets and satellites use forces to escape the gravitational pull of Earth to go into and explore space. Super-strength magnets are being developed that could power the cars of the future, instead of gasoline. Wind turbines and hydroelectric power plants harness natural forces to generate electricity.

From the small-scale forces that enable our daily lives, to the powerful, Earth-shaping forces of plate tectonics, earthquakes, and volcanic eruptions, forces are all around us. With our increased knowledge and understanding of forces and how they work, an exciting future full of possibilities awaits.

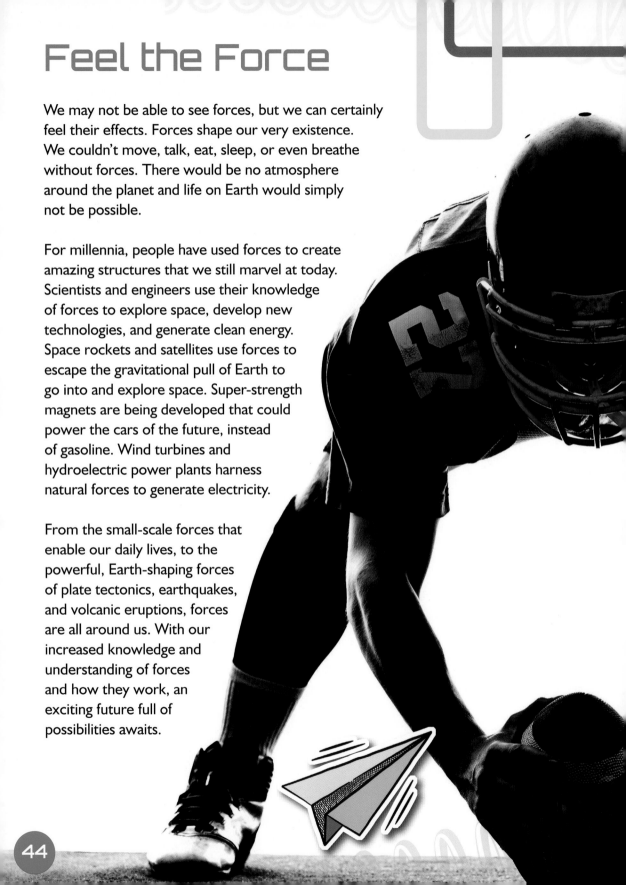

Get Smart!

Understanding forces better can mean the difference between winning and losing. Sports scientists have an extensive knowledge of how muscles use forces and react to training. This means that precise training programs can be made for individual athletes to help them run faster or for longer, or jump farther or higher. Better understanding of aerodynamics is helping cyclists travel more quickly as bikes are redesigned and rider positions adjusted.

Many football players now wear helmets containing single-pole magnets. It's hoped that repelling forces in the helmets will reduce head injuries such as concussions.

Glossary

aerodynamics the study of the way in which objects move through air

balanced forces when two forces are equal and acting in opposite directions on an object

counterweights a weight that provides a balance against something of equal weight

displaced to be moved physically out of position

drag resistant force exerted by air or water on an object

electromagnets objects that become magnetic when an electric current is passed near or through them

energy the ability of an object or material do to work, such as to cause movement

equilibrium a state of balance

escape velocity the speed needed to escape Earth's gravitational pull

forces pushes or pulls

gravitational pull the natural attraction between all objects, large or small

hydroelectric power energy harnessed from moving water

jib the horizontal loading arm of a crane

loads the weights carried or supported by a structure

magma the molten rock underground

magnetic field the area around a magnet in which its pull can be felt

mass the quantity of matter that an object or material contains

matter the substance that makes up any object or material

mechanical advantage using pulleys and ropes to enable the moving of an object using less force

pumice a lightweight, porous volcanic rock formed when frothy lava solidifies

rotation the act of turning or spinning

streamlined smooth and sleek, and not causing much resistance in air or water

strength how strong or powerful something is

tectonic plates the enormous pieces of Earth's crust

transverse waves waves in which the forces move at right angles to the direction of the waves

tread the pattern of raised lines on the surface of a tire that help improve grip

unbalanced forces two forces that are not equal or act in opposite directions on an object

volcanic vent weak area in Earth's crust from which magma can escape

weight the force exerted on a mass by a gravitational field

For More Information

Books

Hollihan, Kerrie Logan. *Isaac Newton and Physics for Kids*
(For Kids). Chicago, IL: Review Press, 2009.

TIME For Kids Big Book of Science Experiments.
New York, NY: Time For Kids, 2011.

Woodford, Chris, and Steve Parker. *Science, A Visual Encyclopedia*. New York,
NY: DK Children, 2014.

Websites

Find fascinating information on all aspects of science at the American Museum
of Natural History website:
amnh.org

Check out more facts about magnets and magnetic fields at:
**education.nationalgeographic.com/education/encyclopedia/
magnetism/?ar_a=1**

Watch live volcanoes erupt online at the Hawaiian Volcano Observatory
website:
hvo.wr.usgs.gov

Learn all about gravity at this NASA page:
spaceplace.nasa.gov/what-is-gravity/en

Index